HOW COMPUTERS WORK

NANCY DICKMANN

Gareth Stevens
PUBLISHING

1010101
10101

Please visit our website, www.garethstevens.com.
For a free color catalog of all our high-quality books,
call toll free 1-800-542-2595 or fax 1-877-542-2596.

Cataloging-in-Publication Data

Names: Dickmann, Nancy.
Title: How computers work / Nancy Dickmann.
Description: New York : Gareth Stevens Publishing, 2020. | Series: Computing for kids |
Includes glossary and index.
Identifiers: ISBN 9781538252581 (pbk.) | ISBN 9781538252598 (library bound)
Subjects: LCSH: Computers--Juvenile literature. | Computer science--Juvenile literature. |
Electronic digital computers--History--Juvenile literature.
Classification: LCC QA76.52 D49 2020 | DDC 004--dc23

Published in 2020 by
Gareth Stevens Publishing
111 East 14th Street, Suite 349
New York, NY 10003

For Brown Bear Books Ltd:
Text and Editor: Nancy Dickmann
Children's Publisher: Anne O'Daly
Design Manager: Keith Davis
Designer and illustrator: Supriya Sahai
Picture Manager: Sophie Mortimer
Concept development: Square and Circus

Printed in the United States of America

CPSIA compliance information: Batch #CS20GS: For further information contact
Gareth Stevens, New York, New York at 1-800-542-2595.

Picture credits: Front cover: Shutterstock;
Interior: Dreamstime: Syda Poductions 5;
iStock: Tevarak 21; Public Domain: 25, Mr John
Cummings 11; Shutterstock: Avava 6, Billion
Photos 13, Bloomicon 9, Bplanet 19, Daniel
Chetoni 27, Forgem 24, Freeograph 4, Antonio
Guillem 12, Kanynov 20, N Ketsunthon 7,
Anatolli Lagunov 23, Monkey Business Images
17, Virginia Obada 22, Andrey Popov 16,
SerPHoto 18, Fabrika Simf 10, Melody Smart 8,
Sirikorn Thamiyom 15, Tommy Lee Walker 26,
WaveBreakMedia 14.

Words in the glossary appear in bold type
the first time they are used in the text.

{ }

CONTENTS

COMPUTERS ALL AROUND US

You can find computers everywhere around you. They come in all different shapes and sizes!

Big computers do complicated jobs. They can predict the weather or fly **virtual** aircraft. There are smaller personal computers too. People use them at home. There are also computers inside some toys and gadgets.

Many people use computers for work.

4

Mini computers

You probably use smartphones or tablets every day. These devices are really just mini computers. They have many of the same parts as a laptop. They can do many of the same jobs.

The first personal computers were introduced in the 1970s.

Tablets are great for playing games or working on school projects.

WHAT IS A COMPUTER?

A computer is a type of machine. Computers can do lots of jobs.

Computers can store **data** (information) and retrieve it (find it again) later. They can follow instructions and look for patterns in data. You can use computers to type reports, play games, or send messages.

An MP3 player has a simple computer that lets you choose which songs to play.

Your brain works a bit like a computer, but it is much more creative.

Computers vs brains

It is easy to think that computers are supersmart. They are great at figuring out complex problems. But they don't have a brain. Computers can't have their own ideas. They can only follow the instructions they are given.

Powerful computers can be taught to play games like chess. They can sometimes beat human experts!

RUNNING PROGRAMS

To do any job, a computer has to follow instructions. These instructions are called a **program**.

All computers come with a program called the **operating system**. This is the most important program that the computer runs. The operating system tells the computer how to get its parts working together. It controls the windows, menus, and icons.

A computer program can have millions of lines of instructions.

Applications

You can install other programs on a computer, such as games and internet browsers. These are called applications, or apps. They don't usually come with the computer. You can decide which applications you want to add.

People called coders write computer programs. They use many different programming languages.

Each app on a smartphone or tablet is a separate computer program.

THE FIRST COMPUTERS

Today's computers are much more powerful than the earliest versions. We have come a long way!

The first computers were really just simple calculators. They used **cogs** and wheels to add and subtract numbers. They couldn't run programs. In the 1800s, Charles Babbage designed the first computer that could be programmed.

The abacus was invented thousands of years ago. It is the earliest form of computer.

Babbage's computer

Babbage's invention was called the Analytical Engine. He could give it instructions using cards with holes punched in them. The machine would solve complicated math problems and print out the answer. But Babbage never finished building it. It was too big and expensive.

In the past, some people were called "computers." They figured out complicated math problems.

Babbage built a trial model of part of the Analytical Engine.

TYPES OF COMPUTERS

A desktop computer is too big to carry around with you.

Some computers can fill a whole room! The computers that you use at home and school are much smaller.

A desktop computer often has a large box that is connected to a **monitor**. In some desktop computers, the box and monitor are combined into one. A laptop computer is smaller. It flips open, like a book. A laptop is light and **portable**.

Tablets are easy to use on the go. You don't even need a lap!

Small computers

Tablets are smaller than laptops. They use a **touchscreen**, so you can tap and swipe instead of using a mouse. Some tablets are the size of a paperback book. Smartphones are even smaller. They are also computers!

Apple's famous iPad tablet was first sold in 2010.

INPUT AND OUTPUT

A computer must be able to receive and send out information. This is called **input** and **output**.

An input device is a tool that lets us give a computer information or instructions. A keyboard is an input device. So is a mouse. Microphones and webcams are also input devices.

When you type on a keyboard, that information gets sent to the computer.

Output devices

A computer sends information to an output device. One of the most important output devices is a monitor or screen. It displays the computer's information. A printer is also an output device. So are speakers.

A projector is an output device. It can display pictures on a whiteboard.

Headphones are another type of output device. You can plug them into a computer or tablet.

COMPUTER SCREENS

Without a screen, computers would be almost impossible to use.

A computer's screen shows you what the computer is doing. The computer displays **documents** and windows on the screen. A computer screen can be a separate piece of equipment called a monitor. It can also be built into the computer, like the screen on a laptop.

Modern computer monitors look a lot like televisions. In fact, you can use a television as a computer monitor!

Touchscreens

Some computers have touchscreens. By tapping, swiping, and pinching, you can input instructions. Then the screen displays the output! Tablets and smartphones have touchscreens. Some laptops have them as well.

In the past, computer screens were black and green. Now they are in full color.

This boy is using a **stylus** to control the touchscreen. You can also use your fingers.

PARTS OF A COMPUTER

A rubber case gives a tablet extra protection, in case you drop it.

Have you ever looked inside a computer? They have many different parts.

Computer designers find a way to fit all the parts together. Many of the electronic parts are delicate. They need a hard outer shell for protection. The outside of a computer is usually made of hard plastic or metal.

A fan pulls cool air into a computer. It helps blow warm air away.

Cooling down

When a computer runs, it produces heat. Too much heat can damage the computer's delicate parts. Many computers have **heat sensors**. They can tell if the computer is getting too hot.

Desktop computers have fans that blow air to keep things cool. Some laptops and tablets also have fans.

THE MOTHERBOARD

A motherboard holds the computer's complex electronic parts in place.

There is a **motherboard** inside every computer. The different electrical parts are all connected to the motherboard. This allows them to work together. **Circuits** called "buses" connect the different parts.

These lines on the motherboard are circuits. They connect different parts to each other.

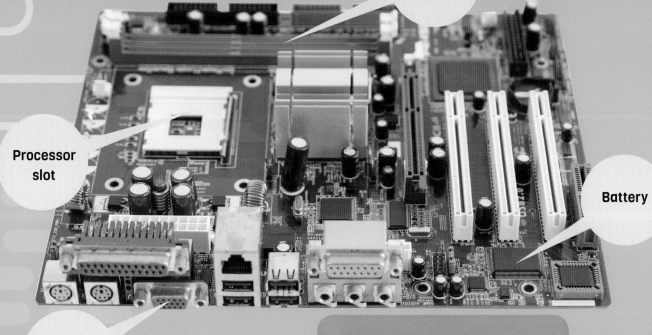

Memory slot

Processor slot

Battery

Connector slots

The battery, **memory**, and **processor** are all on the motherboard.

On board the motherboard

Many motherboards are green.
They can also be blue, red, or yellow.
When you buy a computer, it comes
with all the main parts already
fitted on the motherboard. Other
parts can be added on later.

Motherboards
are a kind of PCB,
short for "printed
circuit board."

CENTRAL PROCESSING UNIT

The CPU is attached to the motherboard, where it connects to other parts.

The Central Processing Unit (**CPU**) is the most important part of any computer.

Just like your brain is the control center for your body, the CPU controls the rest of the computer. It sorts and searches data. It does calculations. The CPU is involved in anything that you do on the computer.

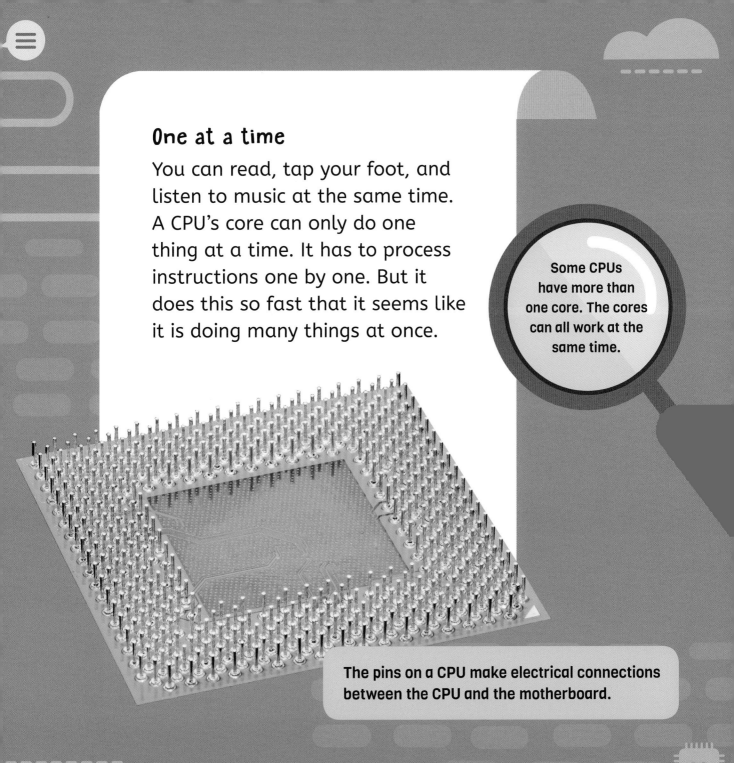

One at a time

You can read, tap your foot, and listen to music at the same time. A CPU's core can only do one thing at a time. It has to process instructions one by one. But it does this so fast that it seems like it is doing many things at once.

Some CPUs have more than one core. The cores can all work at the same time.

The pins on a CPU make electrical connections between the CPU and the motherboard.

MEMORY AND POWER

One of a computer's most important jobs is storing data.

RAM is one of the main types of computer memory. It is a **chip** that attaches to the motherboard. RAM stores data while the CPU is working on it. Your files are saved on a hard drive. This is called storage. It is different from memory.

You can also store documents and photos on a flash drive.

You can recharge batteries without plugging them in. A solar charger captures energy from the sun to recharge batteries.

Solar charger

Power up!

Computers need electricity to run. Desktop computers plug into an outlet, so they have to stay in one place. Laptops and tablets have batteries. A battery will last for several hours. You plug them in when they need recharging.

Old batteries lose their charge faster than new ones.

25

COMPUTER CONNECTIONS

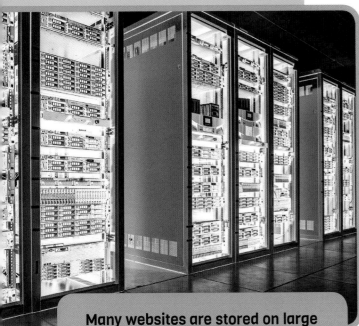

Many websites are stored on large computers in a server farm. Your computer communicates with these to access the website.

Computers are most useful when they can connect to other computers.

Computers connect so they can share information. When you look at a website, your computer is communicating with the computer where the website is stored. A computer can also connect with other devices in your home, such as a television.

Wires and wireless

Sometimes computers connect using cables. Electric signals travel along the cable. Other connections don't need wires. This is called Wi-Fi. Electric signals travel through the air as invisible waves.

A smartphone can connect to the internet using a cell phone signal.

Some cables use superthin strands of glass to send pulses of light.

QUIZ

Try this quiz and test your knowledge of computers! The answers are on page 32.

1. What is a computer program?

a. a class where people learn about computers

b. a list of instructions for a computer to follow

c. a really boring TV show that just shows a picture of a computer

2. What job does a coder do?

a. writes computer programs

b. composes secret messages for spies

c. takes computers apart and puts them back together

3. What did Charles Babbage invent in the 1800s?

a. a new and tasty method of cooking cabbage

b. the smartphone

c. the first computer that could be programmed

4. What type of device is a keyboard?

a. input

b. output

c. shotput

5. What's so special about a touchscreen?

a. it's made from thinly sliced diamonds

b. it can be used for input as well as output

c. it can recharge a tablet's battery using sunlight

6. Why does a desktop computer need a fan?

a. to keep flies and mosquitoes away

b. to maintain its self-esteem

c. to keep its delicate electrical parts from overheating

7. How are the parts on a motherboard connected to each other?

a. using circuits called "buses"

b. with fiber-optic cables

c. with strands of superthin spaghetti

8. What is a server farm?

a. a chip that attaches to the motherboard

b. a large collection of powerful computers where data is stored

c. a field where microchips are planted to grow into computers

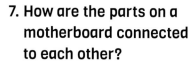

GLOSSARY

chip a tiny wafer of material inside a computer that contains electrical circuits

circuits paths around which an electrical current can flow

cogs moving wheels or bars with parts sticking out from the edges that engage with other parts

CPU (short for central processing unit) the central part of a computer where operations are controlled and carried out

data information that is stored or used in a computer, in the form of a series of ones and zeroes

documents files made by a computer that contain information in the form of text, sound, or images

heat sensors devices that measure heat

input something that is put into a system, such as information that is sent to a computer

memory the part of a computer where data or instructions are stored

monitor a screen that displays an image produced by a computer

motherboard a printed circuit board that contains and connects all the main components of a computer

operating system the program that controls a computer's basic functions and keeps its parts working together

output something that is sent out of a system, such as information that a computer sends out

portable small, light, and easy to carry around

processor the part of a computer that carries out basic instructions

program a set of coded instructions for a computer to follow

stylus a tool that looks like a pen with a soft tip that can be used to write or draw on a touchscreen

touchscreen a display screen that lets a user interact with the computer by touching areas on the screen

virtual not real

FIND OUT MORE

Books

Beevor, Lucy. *The Invention of the Computer (World-Changing Inventions)*. Mankato, MN: Capstone Press, 2018.

Gifford, Clive. *The Science of Computers (Get Connected to Digital Literacy)*. New York: Crabtree Publishing Company, 2015.

Liukas, Linda. *Hello Ruby: Journey Inside the Computer*. New York: Fiewel and Friends, 2017.

Zuchora-Walske, Christine. *What's Inside My Computer? (Lightning Bolt Books – Our Digital World)*. Minneapolis, MN: Lerner Publications, 2015.

Websites

Go here to find answers to questions about computers:
www.bbc.com/bitesize/subjects/zyhbwmn

Learn more details about how computers work:
www.explainthatstuff.com/howcomputerswork.html

This article has more information about personal computers:
computer.howstuffworks.com/pc.htm

Visit this site to learn more about touchscreens:
wonderopolis.org/wonder/how-do-touch-screens-work

INDEX

Quiz answers
1. b; 2. a; 3. c; 4. a; 5. b; 6. c; 7. a; 8. b